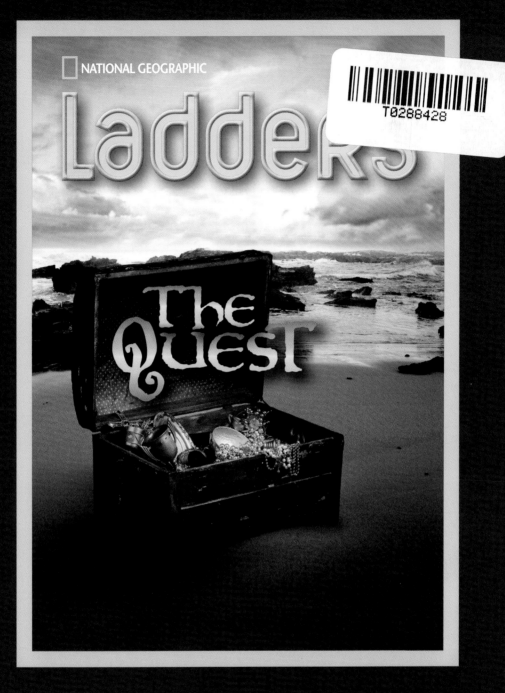

NATIONAL GEOGRAPHIC

Ladders

The Quest

T0288428

JASON AND THE GOLDEN FLEECE

RETOLD BY
ANNE KASKE

ILLUSTRATED BY
MARCELO BAEZ

JASON

LEADER OF THE
QUEST FOR THE
GOLDEN FLEECE

HERCULES

MEMBER OF THE
CREW, NOTED FOR
HIS GREAT STRENGTH

HERA

GODDESS WHO
GUIDES THE QUEST
FOR THE GOLDEN
FLEECE

KING PELIAS

(PEE-LEE-US)
JASON'S UNCLE,
RULER OF IOLCUS

KING AEETES

(EE-EE-TEZ)
RULER OF COLCHIS,
HOME OF THE
GOLDEN FLEECE

MEDEA

(MI-DEE-UH)
DAUGHTER OF
KING AEETES

TWENTY YEARS BEFORE THIS STORY BEGAN, THE EVIL PELIAS STOLE THE THRONE FROM HIS BROTHER, THE RIGHTFUL KING OF IOLCUS. PELIAS THOUGHT ALL OF HIS OTHER RELATIVES WERE DEAD, INCLUDING HIS NEPHEW JASON. NOBODY COULD TAKE THE THRONE FROM HIM NOW . . . OR SO KING PELIAS BELIEVED!

HOWEVER, THE FIRST DAY THAT KING PELIAS WORE HIS BROTHER'S CROWN, AN **ORACLE** GAVE HIM AN UNWELCOME PREDICTION: A RELATIVE WITH ONE SANDAL WOULD COME TO END HIS LIFE. AND FOR TWENTY YEARS, KING PELIAS RULED, DREADING THE ARRIVAL OF A STRANGER WITH ONE SANDAL.

BLACK SEA

COLCHIS
(KOHL-KIS)

JASON'S **QUEST** BEGINS AND ENDS HERE.

THE CLASHING ROCKS

ISLAND OF KING PHINEAS

ISLAND OF THE SIRENS

IOLCUS
(YOL-KUS)

ATTACK OF SCYLLA AND CHARYBDIS
(SIL-UH) (KUH-RIB-DIS)

MEDITERRANEAN SEA

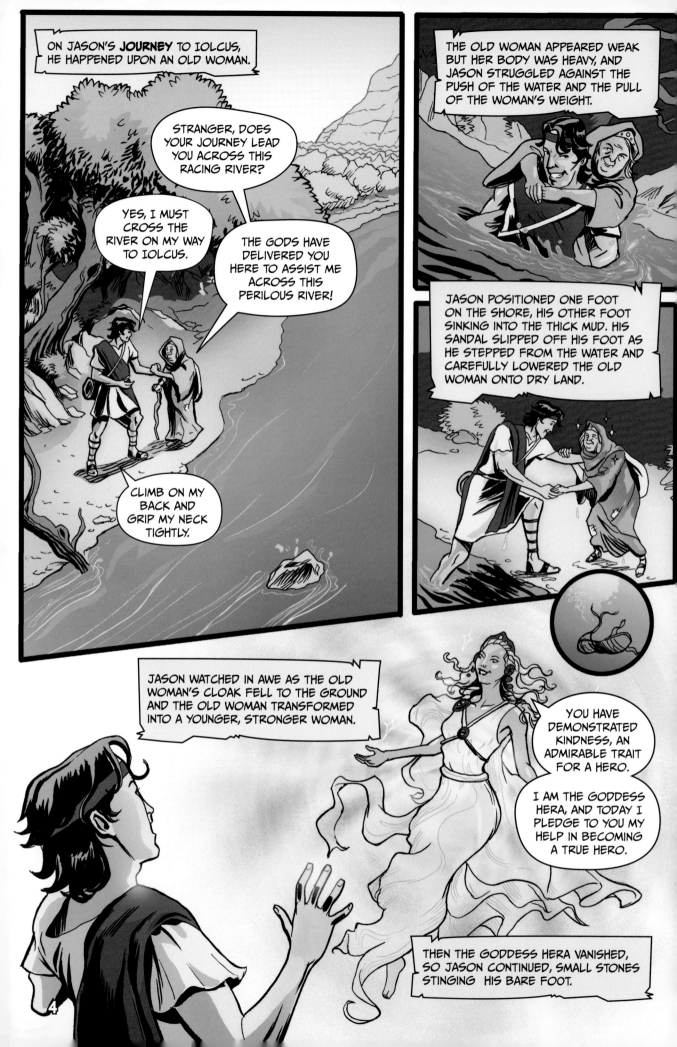

5

JASON ASSEMBLED 49 HEROES TO HELP SAIL THE *ARGO*. THEY INCLUDED ORPHEUS, A GIFTED MUSICIAN WHOSE MUSIC WAS LIKE MAGIC, AND HERCULES, THE STRONGEST AND MOST FAMOUS HERO OF THE LAND. JASON CALLED HIS CREW THE ARGONAUTS.

MY QUEST REQURES INCREDIBLE STRENGTH, SO I ASK YOU, HERCULES, TO LEAD ME.

I HAPPILY OFFER YOU ALL OF MY STRENGTH, BUT IT IS YOUR QUEST, JASON, SO YOU SHALL LEAD.

JASON AND HIS ARGONAUTS WERE SOON PREPARED FOR THEIR JOURNEY, BUT THEY WERE UNSURE OF WHICH DIRECTION TO SAIL UNTIL THEY HEARD HERA'S VOICE . . .

I SPEAK TO YOU FROM THE PROW OF YOUR SHIP TO GUIDE YOU ALONG ON THIS TREACHEROUS TRIP.

HERA, I SEEK THE GOLDEN FLEECE.

VISIT KING PHINEAS FIRST INDEED, FOR NOW IS THE HOUR OF HIS GREATEST NEED.

WITH THE STRENGTH OF THE ARGONAUTS AND HERA'S GUIDANCE, THE *ARGO* GLIDED EFFORTLESSLY INTO THE VAST SEA.

OUT AT SEA, THE HEROES ROWED, CHURNING VIGOROUSLY THROUGH THE FOAMY WATER. IN TIME, ALL OF THE MEN FAINTED FROM EXHAUSTION EXCEPT FOR JASON AND HERCULES. THEY KEPT ROWING, MOVING THE MASSIVE SHIP ACROSS THE WATER.

JASON COLLAPSED AND HERCULES ROWED ALONE WITH HIS MIGHTY ARMS. BUT THEN HIS OAR SNAPPED IN TWO, AND THE *ARGO* COASTED THROUGH THE WATER UNTIL IT STOPPED ON A NEARBY SHORE. HERCULES LEFT THE SHIP TO SEARCH FOR WOOD TO CREATE A NEW OAR, BUT WHEN HE DID NOT RETURN, JASON WAS FORCED TO ABANDON HERCULES AND CONTINUE THE JOURNEY.

CEASE YOUR EFFORTS, JASON, FOR I HAVE ENOUGH STRENGTH TO ROW ALONE!

AT LAST, THE *ARGO* ARRIVED AT AN EERILY QUIET ISLAND THAT WAS RULED BY KING PHINEAS, WHO INVITED THEM TO AN EXTRAVAGANT OUTDOOR BANQUET.

BEFORE THE MEN COULD ENJOY A BITE, ENORMOUS CREATURES SWOOPED OVERHEAD, SNATCHING THE FOOD WITH CURVED, SHARP CLAWS.

FRIENDS, LET US VANQUISH THESE CREATURES!

HARPIES! THEY HAVE CURSED MY TABLE FOR DECADES.

JASON AND THE ARGONAUTS DEFEATED THE HARPIES, AND THE TERRIFYING BIRD-CREATURES RETREATED, THEIR SHRIEKS ECHOING IN THE SKY. KING PHINEAS AND THE MEN RETURNED TO THE BANQUET, ABLE TO ENJOY THE SUMPTUOUS FEAST.

DO NOT TRY, FOR THE CLASHING ROCKS HAVE CRUSHED NUMEROUS SHIPS!

WE HAVE FREED YOU FROM THE HARPIES, SO NOW GUIDE US TO THE GOLDEN FLEECE.

WE ARE NOT AFRAID.

BRAVE MEN CAN STILL DIE! BUT YOU HAVE RESCUED ME FROM STARVATION, SO I WILL HELP YOU. TAKE THIS WHITE DOVE AND FOLLOW IT THROUGH THE CLASHING ROCKS.

THE ARGO DROPPED ANCHOR AT THE PORT OF COLCHIS, A PROSPEROUS KINGDOM ON THE BLACK SEA, AND THE HOME OF THE GOLDEN FLEECE.

KING AEETES AND HIS DAUGHTER, MEDEA, WELCOMED THE HEROES.

I HAVE COME FOR THE GOLDEN **FLEECE.**

NUMEROUS HEROES HAVE ATTEMPTED TO WIN THE FLEECE, BUT ALL HAVE FAILED.

DO NOT ASSUME THAT I WILL JUST OFFER IT TO YOU FREELY!

BUT WE ARE DELIGHTED TO GIVE THIS CANDIDATE AN OPPORTUNITY!

I AM READY TO MEET ANY CHALLENGE YOU MAY ASSIGN TO ME.

TOMORROW AT DAYBREAK, TAME MY WILD BULLS AND USE THEM TO PLOW THE FIELD.

AFTER YOU SOW THESE DRAGON'S TEETH IN THE FIELD, THE GOLDEN FLEECE WILL BE YOURS.

AND WHEN I COMPLETE THE TASK, YOU WILL AWARD ME THE FLEECE?

KING AEETES HANDED JASON THE BAG OF DRAGON'S TEETH AND THEN DISMISSED THE HERO AND HIS CREW FOR THE NIGHT.

9

HERA KNEW THAT MEDEA HAD MAGICAL POWERS THAT WOULD HELP JASON IN HIS QUEST. SO HERA ENCOURAGED CUPID TO SHOOT HIS GOLDEN ARROW AT MEDEA. THE GOLDEN ARROW CAUSED MEDEA TO FALL IN LOVE WITH JASON INSTANTLY.

AT DAWN, MEDEA MET JASON ON HIS WAY TO THE FIELD. SHE OFFERED TO HELP HIM IF HE MARRIED HER AND TOOK HER AWAY FROM COLCHIS. HE AGREED TO MAKE HER HIS QUEEN WHEN HE RETURNED TO IOLCUS.

WHY?

JUST DO AS I SAY!

COVER YOUR SKIN WITH THIS LIQUID.

AS JASON TRIED TO TAME THE RED BULLS, HE DISCOVERED THAT THE BULLS SNORTED RED FIRE!

BUT MEDEA'S MAGIC LIQUID PROTECTED JASON FROM THE BULLS' FIERY BREATH.

JASON HARNESSED THE BULLS AND ATTACHED SILVER PLOWS. HE WALKED BEHIND THE TAME BULLS AND DROPPED THE DRAGON'S TEETH INTO THE SOIL.

THE DRAGON'S TEETH GREW RAPIDLY INTO FEARSOME WARRIORS WITH GLOWING RED EYES!

JASON SEIZED THE FLEECE, AND HE AND MEDEA ESCAPED TO THE *ARGO* TO SAIL HOME TO IOLCUS.

AS THEY PASSED THE ISLAND OF THE SIRENS, THE MEN HEARD SINGING. IT WAS THE SIRENS, CREATURES WHO WERE HALF-WOMAN, HALF-BIRD.

I HEAR NOTHING! WHY DO THE MEN BEHAVE THIS WAY?

THE SIRENS' ENCHANTING SONG LURES THE MEN TO THE ISLAND. WE MUST DISTRACT THEM!

MEDEA FORCED ORPHEUS TO PLAY HIS LYRE TO DROWN OUT THE SIRENS' SONG.

LISTEN TO THE MUSIC ORPHEUS PLAYS!

THE NOTES FROM THE LYRE CIRCLED AROUND THE MEN, AND THE *ARGO* SAILED SAFELY PAST THE SIRENS.

NEXT, THE *ARGO* WAS ATTACKED BY TWO HORRIFYING MONSTERS. SCYLLA HAD DOGS FOR LEGS, AND THEY TRIED TO BITE THE SHIP APART. CHARYBDIS HAD A MOUTH LIKE A WHIRLPOOL THAT TRIED TO SWALLOW THE SHIP.

MEDEA LOVED JASON AND HAD TO STOP KING PELIAS, SO THE NEXT MORNING SHE PAID THE EVIL RULER A VISIT.

KING, IF YOU DRINK THIS, YOU WILL BE YOUNG AGAIN, AND JASON WILL NOT BE ABLE TO FIGHT FOR YOUR THRONE.

WHY WOULD YOU HELP ME?

I DO NOT LOVE JASON, SO MAKE ME YOUR QUEEN, AND MY MAGIC WILL PROTECT YOU FROM HIM.

KING PELIAS GRABBED THE BOTTLE FROM MEDEA AND DRANK IT ALL, IMMEDIATELY COLLAPSING TO THE GROUND.

MEDEA, WHAT HAS HAPPENED?

PELIAS PLANNED TO MURDER YOU, JUST AS HE MURDERED YOUR FATHER, SO I OFFERED HIM A SLEEPING POTION, AND NOW HE WILL SLUMBER FOREVER.

AND SO THE ORACLE'S WORDS HELD TRUTH: A RELATIVE WITH ONE SANDAL ENDED KING PELIAS'S LIFE.

JASON TOOK HIS POSITION AS RIGHTFUL KING OF IOLCUS WITH MEDEA AT HIS SIDE, AND THE GOLDEN FLEECE SHONE IN HIS KINGDOM FOREVER.

Check In What events led Jason on a heroic quest?

15

Dreams of Treasure

retold by Seddie Emerson
illustrated by Annie Wilkinson

There once was a man who toiled every day from sunrise to sunset. His house was worn, but he had no money to repair it. His garden was dry, but he had no time to water it. Day after day, he was so exhausted from working in the hot sun that he would just eat a simple supper and then go directly to sleep.

But he was happy enough with his life. He was able to fill his plate with wilted vegetables from his garden and wrinkled figs from his sickly tree. He slept soundly on a simple bed, although the wind blew in through a hole in the wall and whispered during the night.

One night the man fell asleep to the sound of the wind once again, and he had an unusual dream. The next morning he smiled, for a dream was a ridiculous thing that meant nothing at all. But he dreamed precisely the same dream a second night. The next morning the man smiled and told himself again that a dream was a ridiculous thing to pay attention to. But the man dreamed precisely the same dream a third night! The next morning, he recalled the dream in detail. For three consecutive nights, the man dreamed of a woman in blue hovering above him whispering, "Your **fortune** is in the city."

"Having a dream one night is nothing," the man said to himself as he watched the sun rise. "Having precisely the same dream two nights in a row is peculiar. But having precisely the same dream for three nights warrants my attention!"

So the man sent word to his neighbor that he would be away for a few days. He retrieved a cloth bag from the top of a cabinet and filled it with some meager possessions and the few coins in his money box. Then he started his **journey** to the city in a **quest** for his fortune.

The man arrived at the marketplace in the center of the city, where merchants were busy trading spices, silks, and beads. But the sun would set soon, and he could not hunt for his fortune in the dark.

"I must find a place to sleep tonight," the man said to himself.

Just then, three thieves approached him. Two of the thieves clutched his arms while the third snatched his bag. As the criminals ran away, the man sank to his knees, realizing that he had no money for a room. But he saw a fountain, noticed the smooth stone beside it, and decided it would be an acceptable place to pass the night. He stretched out next to the fountain and shut his eyes.

The next morning the sun tickled the man's face, and as he opened his eyes, he beheld the stern face of a police **official.**

"What is your reason for sleeping outside?" the official demanded.

"Sir, I beg forgiveness," the man apologized earnestly, "but I was robbed last night by three thieves, and I thought this fountain was a good place to rest."

"You are not a citizen of this city," the official bellowed, "so explain to me what business brought you here!"

"I am here to seek my fortune," the man declared.

"And what makes you think you will find your fortune in the city?" the official demanded.

"A woman in blue told me so in a dream," the man explained simply and honestly.

The official's reaction astonished the man—the official howled with laughter and then said with amusement, "People do not heed dreams! In fact, I had a dream just last night. I've had the same dream three times now!"

The official told the man about his dream in detail. In the official's dream, he saw a dry garden with wilting vegetables and a sickly fig tree. A woman's voice suggested he go to a worn house in the country with such a garden and dig beneath the fig tree. There, he would discover a large and amazing **treasure.**

The official laughed, "I'm not going to make a long journey to the country just because of a ridiculous dream!"

As the official teased the man for traveling to the city to pursue a dream, the man reflected.

"I have a worn house," the man thought to himself," and I have a dry garden with a sickly fig tree."

"Oh!" the man exclaimed as he realized that the treasure was at his own house!

"What?" the official asked in response to the man's outburst.

The man looked down to conceal his smile and said meekly, "You're right. I'll be on my way."

The official sighed and offered the man a coin. "Use this to buy food for your journey," he ordered, adding, "And do not pursue any more worthless dreams."

The man purchased food with the official's coin and then took the fastest route home, where he grabbed his shovel and proceeded to dig. He continued digging into the night until he found his fortune. He sent some gold to the police official in the city and then whispered thanks to the woman in blue who had appeared to him in the dreams.

Now the man had money to repair his worn house, but he only used a little of his treasure and saved the rest. He no longer toiled from sunrise to sunset, so he had time to tend his garden. He spent his evenings sharing meals of fresh vegetables and figs with his neighbors. By the end of each day, he fell peacefully to sleep. He was happy enough with his life.

Check In How did dreams lead the poor man on a quest?

GEOCACHING

by Anthony Tibbs

A High-Tech Treasure Hunt

You may know about **treasure** hunts that took place in the past or in movies, stories, or video games, but did you know that treasure hunts exist today? Many people around the world participate in **geocaching,** a high-tech treasure-hunting game. *Geo* means "Earth" and *cache* means "hiding place" or "something that is hidden," so a geocache is a treasure that is hidden outside. Geocachers use technology to locate the treasure. Simply follow the step-by-step instructions on these pages, and you can be a geocacher, too!

What You Need

- Internet access
- a GPS device or a GPS-enabled mobile phone
- an adult

This group begins a geocaching adventure by logging on to the geocaching Web site.

Step 1: Go Online

Begin the **quest** online by logging on to the geocaching Web site, registering, and looking for geocache locations in your neighborhood. Choose one that's right for you, then look for its **coordinates** on the Web site. Coordinates are a set of numbers that identify a location on a map or a graph. In geocaching, the coordinates are the latitude and longitude for the location of the geocache.

Latitude and Longitude

The coordinates of the red dot on the map are 30 degrees north latitude and 90 degrees west longitude.

Longitude is distance east or west of the Prime Meridian. Longitude lines are vertical.

Latitude is distance north or south of the Equator. Latitude lines are horizontal.

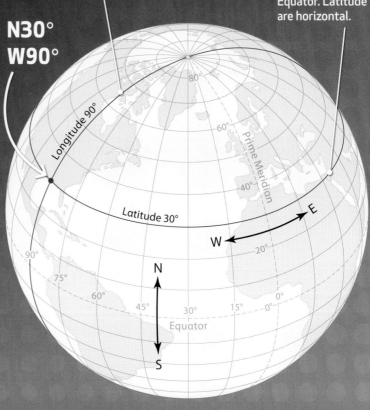

N30°
W90°

Step 2: Get There

Next, enter the coordinates into a GPS device or a GPS-enabled mobile phone. Then follow the directions provided by the GPS device or phone and determine the best way to get to the geocache location—on foot, by bike, or by car. Then go!

GPS-enabled mobile phone

The geocachers use teamwork and technology to zero in on a geocache location.

GPS Technology

GPS stands for Global Positioning System. This system helps people navigate, or get from one location to another.

Satellites in space send signals to a receiver on Earth, such as a GPS-enabled phone. The device in the phone receives the signals then uses them to identify a location.

Directions to the location are shown on the GPS device.

Satellite

Receiver

Step 3: Look Around

You've followed the directions and have successfully arrived at the geocache location, but your quest isn't finished yet! Although most GPS devices can lead you close to the treasure, they can't actually detect the geocache for you. You need to rely on your observation skills, not technology, to finish the hunt.

What kind of object are you looking for? A geocache is a waterproof container that could be as small as your little finger or as large as a trashcan. It's likely to be cleverly concealed and could even be camouflaged to blend in with the environment.

If you search for a long time but are still unable to find the geocache, return to the Web site and read the hints provided by other geocachers.

27

Step 4: Open It!

Congratulations on your discovery! Now that you've finally found the geocache, open it and examine the much-anticipated treasure. According to geocaching rules, if you like the treasure you can take it, but you must replace it with an object of equal or greater value. If you don't like it, simply return it to the container.

The team found the geocache. It is a waterproof container with a tight-fitting lid.

Most geocache containers have just one treasure, but this one has many.

You might find useful objects.

You might find toys and trinkets.

You might find things to wear or collect.

Kinds of Treasure

What kinds of treasure will you find? Most geocache containers are small, so most treasures are small, too.

Step 5: Record

Next, remove the logbook. A logbook is a place to record information about a **journey** or a series of events. Record important statistics, including your geocaching name, the date, and the time of day that you found the geocache. If there's enough space, you can also record details about your experience and describe or draw a picture of the treasure. When you're finished, put the geocache back exactly as you found it—in the same location and position.

Members of the team add their geocaching names, the date, and the time, to the logbook.

5/14/12 - Jenn "the sleuth" Noon
5/15/12 10am pm
Great cache!
4/29/12 - Lucia 29 4:30pm
4/29/12 - Qassim 4:30pm
4/29/12 - Gillie girl 4:30pm
Thanks for the cache!

The team works together to write about their geocaching adventure in the online log.

Step 6: Log Your Find

The adventure isn't over when you discover the treasure.

 **Geocaching Statistics**

GEOCACHING.COM

5 million

About 5 million people in over 100 countries participate in geocaching.

7 continents

There are over 1,300,000 active geocaches around the world. They are on all seven continents. That includes Antarctica!

May, 2000

The first geocache was hidden in May of 2000. It was in the state of Oregon.

Now it's time to look forward to your next geocaching adventure. If you're like most geocachers, acquiring a toy, a trinket, or another treasure isn't what motivates you to participate in geocaching. For most geocachers, the real "treasure" is having an adventure, enjoying the outdoors, and being part of community that likes to explore, too.

Check In How can technology be used in a quest?

Discuss | Compare and Contrast Quests

1. Compare the reasons why Jason and the poor man went on quests. How were their reasons alike and different?

2. Compare the events in Jason's and the poor man's quests. How were the events alike and different?

3. How might modern technology, such as a GPS device, have changed Jason's quest?

4. How are geocachers similar to or different from the treasure seekers in the other two stories?

5. Compare and contrast a quest you have had or have heard about with one of *The Quest* selections.